T0064107

BOZO'S
LEARNINGS

Bozo's Learnings

Good Manners

Pooja Kashyap Chandra

ILLUSTRATED BY
PRACHI KASHYAP
&
AYUSH KASHYAP

PARTRIDGE
A Penguin Random House Company

To order additional copies of this book, contact
Partridge India
000 800 10062 62
orders.india@partridgepublishing.com

www.partridgepublishing.com/india

Dedicated to my Son,
Vagish Viraj Chandra

BOZO GOES TO SCHOOL

Mama – "Wake up Bozo. You have to go to school today."

Bozo – "Good morning Mama. Mama, what the school is like?"

Mama – "School will be a fun Bozo. Get ready now."

Teacher – "Welcome to the school, Bozo."

Teacher – "Come on children, let's sing rhymes."

"Twinkle twinkle little star"

Teacher – "Children! Do you like stories!
Today I'll tell you a story. Once upon a time..."

Bozo – "Mama was right. School is fun."

Teacher – "Wash your hands children. It's time for lunch now."

Teacher – "It's play time children."

Pooja Kashyap Chandra

Students enjoyed playing music on different musical instruments

Teacher – "Come on children. It's time to go home now. See you all tomorrow again. Bye."

Students – "Bye Ma'am"

Mama – "How was the school Bozo?"

Bozo - "Fun. I enjoyed very much Mama."

BOZO LEARNS CLEANLINESS

Bozo: "wow! Yummy!"

Keeping aside the spoon, Bozo started eating with his hands

After he finished eating, Bozo hurriedly ran to play with his toys

Pooja Kashyap Chandra

Mama - "Bozo wash your hands first, then touch your toys, otherwise they will get dirty."

Bozo - "no Mom, they won't."

Mama – "and if they get dirty, I won't buy you any new toy."

Ignoring what Mama said, Bozo began playing with his toys

After a while, Bozo felt sleepy and he slept amidst his toys

After some time, Bozo woke up crying

Mama – "what happened Bozo?"

Bozo – "mama they are biting me. Where did all the ants come from?"

Mama – "see Bozo, I told you to wash your hands after eating, but you didn't listen to me. Ants love sweet taste. Look they are everywhere. The ants have spoiled your toys too."

Mama – "wash your hands before eating. Wash your hands after eating. Wash your hands when you come home."

Bozo – "ok Mama, I will never do this again, I will always wash my hands."

BOZO LEARNS
SHARING

Bozo – "I'll play with my new bat & ball today."

Bruno – "Hi Bozo! You have a new bat & ball. Can we play with you?"

Bozo – "No. This is my bat & ball. Only I'll play with this."

Jill – "But it is much more fun if we play together."

Bozo – "No. You all cannot play with me."

Ribbit – "You are being selfish Bozo. Come friends, let's play our game."

All the other animals follow Ribbit, the tortoise.

Bozo starts playing alone with his new bat and ball

Playing alone bores Bozo, he goes back to his friends hearing their joyful sounds.

Jenn – "Honey Bee, you are hiding behind the tree. Bruno, come out of the bushes..."

Bozo – "Friends! Can I play with you all?"

Bruno – "How can you play with us Bozo?
Remember, you didn't let us play with you."

Bozo – "I'm sorry Bruno. I won't be selfish now. Let's all play with the bat & ball together."

Bozo joyfully plays cricket with all his friends and he understands the importance of sharing.

BOZO LEARNS TO BE REGULAR

Bozo comes home from school and throws his bag and water bottle

Mama – "Bozo! Learn something from Rose. Keep your things on their place."

Bozo ignored what Mama said, and started watching television

Mama – "Rose, Bozo! Come for lunch."

Mama – "After your lunch, finish your home work."

Pooja Kashyap Chandra

Bozo gets tired of watching TV for too long

Bozo – "Mama, I'm going out to play with friends."

Bozo – "Ohh it's so dark. It seems everybody has gone back to their homes."

Bozo – "Mama, there was no one in the field. All my friends went home."

Mama – "Bozo! You must do everything in proper way. You should mend your ways."

Pooja Kashyap Chandra

Next morning waking up late makes Bozo run here and there to get his things.

Bozo – "Mama! Where are my tie & belt?"

Mama – "I asked you to keep your things on place Bozo. But you never listen to me."

Teacher – "Look at the time Bozo! You are too late. And where are your tie and belt?"

Teacher – "Bozo, you have not done your home work also. Get out of the class."

Bozo – "Mama, my teacher scolded me today. My friends were laughing at me."

Mama – "This happened because you were irregular. Listen to what elders say. Obey them & all will be fine."

Bozo – "I am sorry mama. I will always listen to the elders."

BOZO LEARNS
TO WIND UP

Bozo sitting on the floor & playing with toys kept all around him.

Bozo – "Uhh! Had enough of toys. Now I'll watch T.V."

Leaving all his toys on the ground itself,
Bozo sits on the couch and starts watching
television.

Mama – "Bozo! Keep your toys aside first."

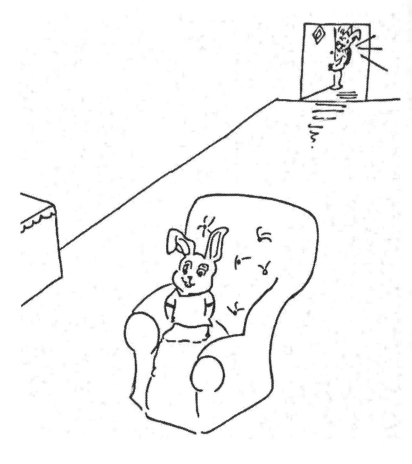

Mama – "Bozo, open the door. Look who has come."

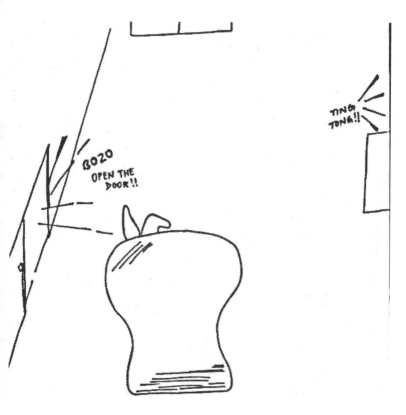

Bozo – "yes mama."

Bozo's Learnings

Rose – "Bozo! Stop laughing. I'm hurt. Why don't you keep your toys on place?"

Leaving Rose fallen on the ground, he again goes to watch T.V.

Bozo – "Mama, I'm going out to play with friends."

Bozo's leg gets entangled in his toys and he falls down.

Bozo – "Mama..."

Doctor – "Leg is fractured."

Mama – "I hope you have learnt the lesson Bozo. Always keep things on their places."

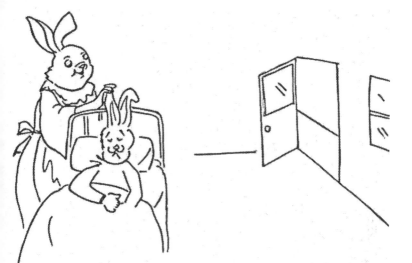

Bozo – "Yes Mama. I'll always listen to you."

BOZO TELLS
THE TRUTH

Bozo's Learnings

Bozo – "Rose have you seen my Art book?"

Rose - "no Bozo, I haven't"

Rose – "Have you lost it Bozo? I'll help you in searching that."

Bozo – "Thank you Rose."

Rose – "Bozo, I'm looking this side, you check in Mama's room."

Bozo – "ok."

Bozo was looking for his book in mama's room. But the vase kept on Mama's table somehow unknowingly gets pushed by Bozo's hand & breaks into pieces.

Bozo is startled & scared.

Mama – "Rose! Bozo! Who broke this flower vase?"

Bozo – "No Mama, I didn't do this.'

Mama – "Ok fine. If you do not tell me the truth, none of you will get your dinner tonight."

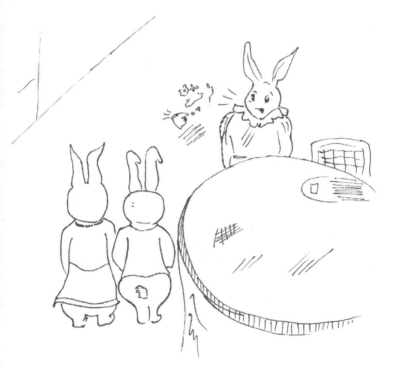

Bozo – "Rose was just helping me. I broke the vase. I must tell Mama, else Rose'll not get her dinner."

Bozo – "I'm sorry Mama. I broke the vase. Let Rose have her dinner. Please do not punish her."

Mama – "You should have told me then itself Bozo. I wouldn't have punished anybody. You should always speak the truth."

Papa – "Bozo! You kept your drawing book in my bag. Take it."

Bozo – "Oh! Thank you Papa."

It left Bozo, Rose and Mama smiling.

Printed in the United States
By Bookmasters